Finding words
for what our life and the day give us
is an act of faith.

Also, by Leonard Neufeldt

Find What Isn't Missing
(Silver Bow Publishing, 2021)
Nearness
(Silver Bow Publishing, 2020)
Figures in Time
(Moonstone Press, 2020)
Painting Over Sketches of Anatolia
(Signature Editions, 2015)
How to Beat the Heat in Bodrum
(Alfred Gustav Press, 2010)
The Coat is Thin
(Cascadia Publishing House, 2008)
Before We Were the Land's
(Horsdal & Schubart, 2002) Heritage Award.
Car Failure North of Nîmes
(Black Moss Press, 1994)
Yarrow
(Black Moss Press, 1993)
Journal Volume 4, The Writings of Henry D. Thoreau
(Princeton Univ. Press, 1992)
Raspberrying
(Black Moss Press, 1991) Lambert Prize shortlist.
The Economist: Henry Thoreau and Enterprise
(Oxford Univ. Press, 1989)
The House of Emerson
(Univ. of Nebraska Press, 1982)
Named "1983 Best Academic Book," (national).
Christian Gauss Prize and Phi Beta Kappa Society shortlist.
A Way of Walking
(Univ. of New Brunswick Press Fiddlehead Series, 1972)

PASSPORT

by

Leonard Neufeldt

720 Sixth St., Box # 5
New Westminster, BC
V3L 3C5 CANADA

Title: PASSPORT
Author: Leonard Neufeldt
Cover Design: "Sun Fog" painting by Candice James
Layout and Editing: Candice James
© 2022 Silver Bow Publishing

ISBN 978177403 200-8(softcover)
ISBN 978177403 201-5(e-book)

All rights reserved including the right to reproduce or translate this book or any portions thereof, in any form without the permission of the publisher. Except for the use of short passages for review purposes, no part of this book may be reproduced, in part or in whole, or transmitted in any form or by any means, electronically or mechanically, including photocopying, recording, or any information or storage retrieval system without prior permission in writing from the publisher or a license from the Canadian Copyright Collective Agency (Access Copyright). Copyright to all individual poems remains with the author.

Library and Archives Canada Cataloguing in Publication

Title: Passport / by Leonard Neufeldt.
Names: Neufeldt, Leonard, author.
Description: Poems.
Identifiers: Canadiana (print) 20220166579 | Canadiana (ebook) 20220166609 | ISBN 9781774032008
    (softcover) | ISBN 9781774032015 (EPUB)
Classification: LCC PS8577.E758 P37 2022 | DDC C811/.54—dc23

In loving memory

Margaret Peters
Lois Rudnick
Karin Schöpp

and
Harvey Neufeldt
beautiful soulmate
from our infancy on

Acknowledgements

My gratitude to editors of literary publications in which the following poems have appeared:

Alfred Gustav Press Chapbook Series 16 (December 2016): "The Acropolis of Assos/Behramkale, Turkey"

The American War Against Itself (anthology): "Temper of the Times"

The Disasters of War (anthology): "Abraham Wittenberg"

Hope 2022 (anthology): "Descendant"

Not Our President! (anthology): "Reality Show Samson"

Rhubarb: "Father and Son: Cold War Harmonies"; "Local Television News"

Protest 2021 (anthology): "If You Look That Way"

The Sky Is Falling! The Sky Is Falling (anthology): "Ballad of the Plague Years"; "Fear"

2021 Featured Poets (anthology): "Descartes and Rumours of a Plague"

Contents

Beginnings, Endings and Beyond

Yarrow ... 13
Political Campaign in Early Yarrow ...15
Little Shadow Boy ...17
The Child's Shape of Death ...19
Finding a Footing ...21
Opera Hockey ...23
The Age of Wordsworth and Coleridge ...25
Garter Snake and House Cat Facts ...31
Brothers ...35
Parterres ...40
Brahms' *Requiem* ...42
Father and Son: Cold War Harmonies ...45
Natalie Marie ...47

Passport

Passport ...51
Continuum ...53
Descendant ...58
Abraham Wittenberg ...59
Exodus ...60
Learning Turkish ...63
The Cow of Good Fortune: A Prose Poem on Non-Fiction ...65
Inventory ...69
The Acropolis of Assos/Behramkale, Turkey ...72
The Bosporus ...74
Amazons ...77

As If

"We Strongly Prefer Experimental Verse" ...83
Local Television News ...84
Boredom ...86
Descartes and Rumours of a Plague ...88
Ode to Horace ...89

Journal of the Plague Years

Fear ...93
Ballad of the Plague Years ...94
Temper of the Times ...95
Reality Show Samson ...96
If You Look that Way ...98
The Quiet of the Field ...99
A Mere Morning Walk ...101

Beginnings, Endings and Beyond

Yarrow

A home of years ago is not itself beholden
to the past like the lichened
outcrops of layered bedrock,
their architecture for a God
of permanent dwelling in a refugee hamlet
and its doctrines of starting over with whatever
has been salvaged and what fields
between wetlands will yield. A village
that couldn't imagine running out of time,
its peacefulness protected by hoods of willows
and regimented rows of poplars.
A boy's loyalties laying hold of what
you knew, even the wind from the Pacific
wandering through hesitant barnyard smells.
The sky a journeying forth of cloud, rain,
hint of rainbow and blue-like departures
beckoning you, that also felt like home
well before you left, before any
dead reckoning could tell you
where you really lived, who you are
or what stays with you after bulldozers
and builders have done their work

The solid feel of the wheel as you take
the old way back into town for a day
that started with a vague desire to be left
alone like the past anxious about
a village that's going the way a body goes

Not the scars of where the Co-op once stood
like a promise to a chosen people,
nor the tire-track circles in a new park
strutted out to meet a visitor's drive-by,
and not the store offering "Whatever
You Need" or the sign to Cultus Lake.
It's not directions that you need now
although the years have renamed the streets,
all of them. And it's not the stir
of remembrance or unlearning
the names. It's the years themselves,

their unfamiliarity, like the point-blank
stare your way of the old man idling
his pickup slowly by,
his mouthed words lost on you although
you learned long ago to read lips

You have been thinking of spent days,
how they veered, how some met with peril,
how you said more than once "I
will arise and go."
Something in you wants to know
what he has done with his life and whether
memory changes us, even if
his words may not be meant for you at all
and he is merely singing of a heaven
of uncomplaining plainness
that never needed to deal with a past,
not even with "When I was younger . . ."
Or are they unforgiving words
for old-timers, those who return
with a high-end jacket over their arm
in order to walk the street and feel neglected?
Perhaps he sees a bony stranger who won't
come back again, will leave no trace
like the heavy exhaust of his truck
circling slowly away. You,
the only one left this Sunday morning
on Yarrow Central Road.
Your visit has no real words. Not yet.
Nor does the house behind you, where
you in your wetness first breathed in
the chill of the world, and the midwife
prophesied of worlds elsewhere,
which she was wont to do

Political Campaign in Early Yarrow

Cowherd leading, the on-time cows
hoofing their near-sighted way
from the common pasture every day
like the history of summer in a village
of refugees who still say
they got to this place by the Almighty's grace.
Their cows an oncoming line or receding
that knows what to want, what to expect,
where to go, like index and pictures
in a mail-order catalogue,
each cow turning in at her gate on her own

Why does the candidate arrive
two hours late and plead
time's incontinence and not his own,
almost bumbling headlong
into a borrowed stick-man lectern,
the village violin teacher's music stand?
And why show up
as though suddenly flushed out of hiding
like the Canada geese,
their faint call through the open door
into this half-lit school basement
of mostly men, slick new concrete floor
and smell of barn and after-shave
betrayed by sweat

The stage small as his prospecting smile.
Two handlers divide themselves
in equal portions before
he begins to hurry us forward
with words on the run
to a hereafter begun
for the first time, promises perched
along the way like strange birds
in a strange tree this seventh day
of the eighth month,
his guttural love of God's pseudonyms
and the great good
tempered by tiredness.

Arms shrinking from exertions
of augury dispatch themselves
as he turns to leave

Broken strings of sound overhead
clearer now, geese calling
the night home

A mere nod of the ushers
and we double-file into the dark,
the day's stiffness of legs and arms
and refusal our assurance
to stay with who we are
by making light of it, familiar
as shared habits of words
and considerations
engaged together like sky,
geese and cropped land, like cowherd
with the women and men leaning
on their gate, their dialect
like the rubato of the night breeze,
a dialect ready to stay an evening,
keep a long life company
but also interrupt a night's sleep
over those who lost track of time,
their last chance staying behind
in the old country.
Dreams of the dead secreted
from losses and lies of the past
that tell the truth
brought here, measured world to world,
still exchangeable

Little Shadow Boy

"Walking before
he learned to crawl."
And one might say the morning sun
laid his shadow down
head to toe next to footprints
in the dew-drenched lawn.
I could write this down,
then scratch it out,
but I'll let myself be
the boy again
with what he finds out

The shadow doesn't move,
and then it does
when he stumbles forward
and down to its dark summons,
to prod it, bury his tiny
index finger in it
and leave words belonging
to him alone

He will let the shadow reach
into him so he can hold it
with both arms,
let it steady him, take it
with him as he tries to stand
and run but slumps again
to knees and hands –
a second invitation
for the shadow to complete
the feeling of its chill
on his arms
now wearing it

He leans back, rubs
his ear, gathers himself,
rises to nowhere until
he sees the closed door,
until he steps back
and to the side. The shadow

is still in front,
still clinging to his feet
although the knob
of his wrist and hand
tell it a word he was taught
Go, stop holding him,
the shadow saying nothing, not even
"don't forget any of this"

There are many things
not written in books,
and there will always be
more than enough
that I don't write about,
so much left behind,
still waiting

The boy is on his knees again

The Child's Shape of Death

There are many boyhoods,
one of the earliest your refusal
to nap. "He won't be three
until the fall," Mother tells rooms
of flowered walls, her words different
this time. She knows
you will go outside
to wander among things of your life

The elephant mountain
is always there, even when it moves
from window to window
and watches you leave the house

Dog barks, his nose down
to the ground ahead of you
under the wings Mother calls
branch or tree. They are larger
than you, larger than big people,
and the bird that knows your song
has been shushed by them

or maybe by the shadows or Mother

You press against Dog, follow him
to your neighbour, Mrs. Froese,
because she always leans down,
touches your chin and hugs you
all the way inside her white apron
and long blue dress

"Onkel Froese has gone to heaven,"
as her hands boost you
up the steps into the room,
lift you to see the bee on his fingers
and kiss his cheek
because he hasn't gone yet,
he's napping in a long bed box,
face scratchy and mouth blue.
Outside she puts you down

in a small shade that watches you
like Dog's ears and eyes when he sleeps,
and she gives you a sugar bun
soft and warm in your mouth.
You hold it with both hands

Dog has gone. "It's time," she says.
The sound of the branches
does not let the bird sing.
The elephant mountain is blue,
and Mother is calling but not
as far off as the mountain,
calling your name.
You will tell her
Onkel Froese is napping now,
but soon he's going to heaven

Boyhoods survive, some by owning
and telling their story,
which is not theirs alone
but a resemblance, its ways trained
on the years coming,
on what they won't leave out

Finding a Footing

He was talking too much about
the take-off point where the stream
was not too deep as he hurried
his shoes off without untying them
and then his clothes, to start across
the narrow wooden dam,
his twiggy shadow shivering light and dark
beyond his feet in the fold
of water rushing to the edge
and over

Devout boys will be surprised as anyone
when there's no bottom, when a body
flails as the dream-reel lays him
courteously out in a coffin, slows
and stops as singers and pastor
are gone like that, crowded pews
no longer meeting his gaze,
the shore, field, woods, horizon afloat,
almost too large for the eye's astonishment
as he finds his windmilling arms.
No end, but a footing becoming as sure
as steps and stumbles forward,
the row of cottonwoods appearing
and reappearing, buoyed by spasms of breath
until body gasps and coughed words
meet his half undressed uncle's stare

"The stream is deeper than I thought
and the dam slippery as oil."
He knew he'd lost his footing
before his jump-off point. He knew
he should have first learned to swim.
He knew that a missing bottom is gurgles
of underwater dark and forgetfulness
that can last forever

Learning isn't fated like that evening
long ago of trying to grasp water
that covered him, and it's not safety's

preserver to go to.
It's an in-between that all these years
has been just ahead or behind like purpose
biding the next close call, and the next,
biding time, always there
with morning light, sometimes tensed
and ready to leap out of dream and sleep
itself, unsure as his footing, sometimes
rich in detail and balanced as awareness
bearing down on the moment, its trueness
not of place but of purchase,
whether it buoys full weight or not

It was merely a swimming hole
in Stewart Creek behind barbed wire,
not hell's freezing river and Dante's
dire posting. People older than him
got baptized there although it was always cold,
and it's still enough, the flow of what was
and what's coming,
learning to find a footing and the feel
of what he's found out,
like the tongue repeating soundlessly
what has just been written
for the first time

Opera Hockey

Hardly Broadway and 40th. Ours
was the smallest show on earth,
the rink a dining room floor cleared of all
but hand-knitted slippers (the game's
surrogate goal posts), the teams
four brothers, two each side
leaning into each other, the crowd
Rossini's *Barber of Seville*
from the packed-in Saturday matinee
at the MET. Our bout of floor polishing
was fully-half-ruled by love of rising
and falling sounds we hadn't known.
The puck a soft plastic readiness,
the polishing cloths outdated red
and brown woolens making up for years
of neglect and moths' quiet ways.
Scoring and arguments over shots
that missed were uneven as the miles
from our torn-out glossies of thoroughbred
New York to the Fraser Valley, and lopsided
as our screech-reach for Roberta Peters'
gift of high Cs and Fs, or our
wall-to-wall delight with Rosina
(Mother turning the radio louder).
We cheered each kick that scored a goal
with raised fist and shout of *Bartolo*
as the floor shuddered its shine

Scoring a goal was easiest when
the other team was doing the singing —
the floor faultless as the sun
emblazoning it by the time the applause
ebbed and Milton Cross marshalled his broad
tenor range over sentence, pause
and tuxedo-perfect pronunciations
to bid us adieu. Our answer transcendental
soprano mimicry as we skated
to our slippers with stubborn joy
that didn't pretend to know one day
the puck would go missing

like a dream one tries at a late breakfast
to remember, afterimage with nothing in it.
Not even a rumour could bring it back
once we began to box our future, take
labels, weight, want and all to the city

Tumult and laughter enough to fill
any space emptied for a morning
or more, and so much song
seeking concert pitch, but the game
was always serious. Sometimes
mannered straight-up pose
or sweeping bow, sometimes a rush,
sometimes a sudden fall
that resonated with the stunned chorus,
the pain all but stopping both skaters
and song, as if the wish to make a lead
in the game insurmountable
might not be granted

Mother looking for a shine smouldering
among soaring arias,
knowing every piece of furniture
would be returned to where it belonged –
each piece the same pattern of solid walnut,
no surprises, not even knots, only
what the makers call 'character'.
An exactness in place and sturdy as what
cannot be dislodged

And yet her voice too finding itself
and singing along with a boy's
overtime in a world of song
so as not to fall out of practice.
Neither dream nor vision
but more and more direct effort
that furthers desire as well as words
not written down, imagines their movement
into a world on the make and much of it
already mostly made like a house emptied
for someone else to own

The Age of Wordsworth and Coleridge

Was it an invitation to complete the day
away from what it had been willing to give?
The comfort of evening when we first tried it?
Our world had an attic that lured two of us
to climb beyond the nine-to-four
hurried humdrum of classroom
or hurt of hard work and harder play
into secret plans in motion and at rest
at the same time, neither cancelling
the other, a freedom of paradox
that overnighted here. Attentions giving way
unwillingly to privacy of sleep
or the night-dream exchange
of half-wakedness over a success
or failure almost weightless,
how its reaction can grow larger, heavier
in the dark unlike Newton's principle
of falling back, more like configurations
and shapes slowly gathering heft
after the light is turned off,
yet free of dead weight like the wonder
of morning come too soon.
Unfinished attic for unfinished youth.
I didn't finish the world I give to you

An attic will talk to itself or us when seasons
change, and one could say what we needed
for company for the evening or night was there,
and what was there was both cause and result
in three seasons and sometimes four
under the slopes of rafters and their
hair-trigger snaps. Vaulted ceiling
and wall one and the same, slat-spaced
horizontals holding cedar shakes
that didn't show their age, the angular
surprise of evenings brought up short
by head-bumps against sloping rafters
we'd ignored in our flashlight guesses
at cardboard cartons and steel drums stored
against the ceiling-wall, those permanent

tenants of mystery and neglect beyond
the reach of a single light bulb hanging
straight down over the double bed
from the ridge beam on a braided chord.
The dimness telling us
the purpose of life is to learn the difference
between light and half-dark and dark

Stranger things are said about places
memorized than places never found,
and we could as easily have slept
in our bedroom of lavender and blue
wallpaper, blond oak floor,
changes of clothes and a low crawlspace
door with a knot that stared at us and moved
when we moved before we fell asleep.
But the bedroom sheltered less of what
we wanted other than daily workouts
on the violin. And to this day
it has less of a past ready to arrive
and less of what stays
like the sure return of the spiderwebs'
sticky weave imperfectly strung
that several times a year we pried off rafters
with a broom grey bearded before we swept
the shiplap floor lengthwise to get
the grooves and all, dust sifting the light.
We didn't get the echo-fed bat
we tried to trap with our top sheet
stretched high as a sail, but our neighbour
rocked on his toes, pistol pointing to where
chimney bricks and centre beam met
in a small darkness only slightly larger
than the bat

Although our village God was carefully kept
under house arrest by foreknowledge
and preordained order from the first
universal word to the end of time,
beginning and outcome certain
as the earth's praise of raspberries
without a summer free of drought

or too much rain that would beard the berries
with mould. A certainty unlike our bodies
or the price of berries and bales of hops,
which like an old story
repeated damage estimates of change,
change sure and capricious
as the next murder mystery by flashlight
into dead of summer night,
the negligent earworm hum
of mosquitoes rising and falling
like the cindery breeze through the open
window from the season-long smoulder
on the upper ridge of Vedder Mountain

A book was a way of seeing, a window
for an unpracticed eye to bring close
an unfamiliar vision trained on distance,
on worlds elsewhere impatient
with the short weeks of summer
as night train whistles stretched themselves
from the valley's other side.
And despite more than two hundred
pages of foretellings, no need
for alarm, not even with the last-page
verdict of surprise or with the sound
of a falling flashlight confused by dawn.
Village librarian, Julia Wittenberg,
didn't know one can be at home
in an attic as much as in a library book.
Yet she kept her weekly count of late returns
of each single file armful of books
with a forgiveness far greater
than our universe

Next to our tottery book towers
Northern Electric radio ads
deferred to heavyweight boxing matches,
opera's barrel-chest baritones,
chorus-backed solos of God with
their soul taps into the by and by,
country's sweet-sour three-chord yowls
of desire and broken promises,

crooners' love warm as mid-summer
or gone bad as berries in a season-long
drought, body jolts
of "Rock Around the Clock," and Mel Allen's
mellow cadences allowing us
to see even more than he did
three time zones away as shadows groped
beyond the infield of Yankee Stadium.
Neither victories nor losses held back
our pillow punches and their intervals
between miles of high hope and outcomes
unexpected or still unknown.
Humming, singing, playing along

The flat staccato beat of winter and spring
rain on all sides of us bore
part of its unrelieved burden
of steady drumming and left part for us.
What were we really thinking as we listened
to the rain? Waiting for it to soften
into a dream? But there were nights
when the moon broke free for
its vast inventory of stars and silhouettes,
and we would wake again in time for
early light through gaping window lace
to show us what a first look seemed to ask
our eyes to create, large-bellied cloud
rushing off, dust of snow in the green
grass, a moment's sunlight shining through
a thin crust of ice at eye level
in the half-full water glass

Images holding on, feeling ahead
like a mountaineer's memoir pages.
The images still with us a lifetime
after we planned to leave with no fallback,
no rope or harness for what might go
wrong. Only vague endorsements
from what we believed about ourselves.
Our house sold for a song not worth
repeating. The homegrown speculator
vowed to anyone paying attention

that he'd finish the attic, but he flipped
the house at a guaranteed worth
to losers lest the market turned cold
before his vow could –
as many others have done
in an immigrant village gone mysterious

     **

Someone far from here is climbing stairs
to the door at the top to stand in the entrance
where presence and absence are more than idea,
where they frame him as he steps inside,
glances both ways: a negotiation
between a world's slow-moving stillness
and voices that echoed here
where things were done. A homelessness
moving like him through an attic, and no one
to ask him who he is, why he has come
or why he has chosen one side and not
the other to keep his head in check along
boxes taped and not taped.
He wonders about this ordinariness.
For whom? Those who own no place?
Not his son, who has moved again
to start counselling others on how to improve
their life, how to secure their days

He follows his need to stop in the half-dark,
reach out and feel forward for outlines
and surfaces run together, reach
into them, pry from concealment
some of what's here, unsure how far
to let it reach into him as he draws
a carton to the window's light as though
to let it help him understand what
he should have known. But he leaves the tape
as it is – what does this room stand for?
distance? the heart-hurt of estrangement?
the mystery of pieces of our life
not abandoned, merely forgotten like
a journal lost years ago, or old hymns

or the many marked books given to others?
Each part seeking more
than extinction; each part a voice
answered, yet that goes unanswered still

Garter Snake and House Cat Facts

Early summer children.
Morning lives and moves here
with crooked smiles
that rouse more than a guess
as our girls, all legs and homely grace,
dispatch themselves through open glass
door, kitchen, dining room and up the stairs,
the taller one with right arm salute
and outsized gold-striped bracelet
on her left arm. So attached, so intimate.
That's got to be Freddy, the garter snake,
about to become another bedroom pet,
guessing as you do with others' lives

But you've also learned to recognize their ways
not to be noticed, ways worth knowing
for their next time on your watch.
An errant notice summons you
to follow their tracks up stairway carpet
to where they sit together on bed edge,
the snake's unhoused wariness staring
into the face of innocence tempting
its tongue flicks only inches away

How to manage an image that shouldn't have dared
to be there, waiting to explain itself
or for you to scrabble for the words?
Since the girls turn to you but do not speak
or change the posture of anything
including the snake, you decide to break
the spell by complimenting lack of fear
of Freddy, which you had taught them
on the back lawn by stretching the frantically
anti-vertical snake out before curling him
on your arm, your blood awakened by
the memory of a boyhood broken snake
fang in your bare foot. There are many kinds
of advice possible in a poem looking back,
advice you can offer seamlessly
before leaving children and a garter snake

with head poised in the air to outstare
even them. But you don't leave,
and what you say is that when Cleo
the cat shares their bed at night
she doesn't sleep like them
but lets the moon make shadows in their room
as she watches for other movement

You say the smallest twitch of toe or foot
will turn her head. You don't tell
how a cat can separate serpentine
lethargy from its fatness and stretch it out
as a gift for the morning
next to their slippers. You steady your voice
by explaining how unusual
restlessness along the baseboard dark
will invite a cat to attack. Cleopatra,
the snake and the girls cannot live
together in a bedroom world

The house listening, the girls' murmurs
rising to litanies of unbearable loss,
the kind you once imagined for the end of days,
but Freddy is saved —
taken in hand close to the edge of the wood
where he knows to wait under the willow
for tent caterpillars passing themselves
and each other down from the sky,
growing larger for a feast's simplicity

and where, two days later the girls
find skull-pulsing shriekfuls of snakelets
stirred to life on the lawn's shag of green
by the bare feet among them. Freddy
is renamed Frederika; they have just remade
the world by turning facts
against themselves, against yours,
against Cleo behind the glass door
in the black flesh of her stare

* *

Questions of before and after. Trying
to explain something, and not
for the first time, something that comes
from where you were later that year,
summer over, the sky impatient with clouds,
the air a different chill than now,
a shiver of dark beginning to seep up
from inside the earth
as tree canopies yellowed downward.
You walked to the willow, the branches
owned for a season by caterpillars already bare.
It may have been after you looked up the tree
and then looked down. Frederika still there
stretched fully out on the brown bark
mulch, pointing away from the tree as she did
the day before when you didn't bend down
to look closely. Perhaps she was headless
then already. No way for you to know.
But on your knees now you could tell
uneven stitch work of bites on her neck,
a design across the space of memory
that will not move. *Hey, just a snake to kill*
the boys behind the dyke would have said,
as they did after they held two snakes by the tail,
snapping them full length forward and back
like a bull whip. Again. Spines giving way,
dividing themselves. Snakes and oaths
whooped casually away. And you
refusing to leave. The trance of reckoning
has lingered on the shortcomings, yours
and your world's. Visible as Frederika's
colours, still a dull black with stripes gold
as your oldest daughter's hair or a harvest moon
coming out of clouds, more visible
than puncture marks beyond the neck.
No thought or word, only a kind of grief
in forgiveness curled up inside you
when you weren't thinking of forgiveness.
A headless snake reaching to your touch,
the ache of something short of foreknowing
not left out. The silence

Most cats die of natural causes, and Cleo's
last litter was gifted in small
cardboard cartons to neighbours also gone
like Cleo. But the watch goes on,
and words know in advance that they will outlive
most of what's expected or isn't, although
you wonder what will be left, what taken

Once there was a snake in the garden.
Once two girls said *we are not afraid*

Brothers

Fly fishing on waters of reflections.
Here, brother, where time had its way
with glaciers, and glaciers had their way
with migrants from the other side,
from far beyond evening, who followed
the coastal narrowness
as the sun rose and eagles readied
talons for the next small flash
near the shore or to steal each other's
satisfaction. Our people too trekked
a narrowness, pushing ahead for those
coming after to follow.
The watch lonelier
back then than for you or me,
who both have travelled far and often into
a world of cities for as long as a month
or year and imagined settling down
elsewhere – the lure. But we always knew
why we packed little more
than we've done to cast about here, not far
from the tombstone fields of stumps
just west of a skyward metropolis
whose hunger gnaws away its outmost self
and dreams of the more it always needs,
mitotic fission of light-rail suburbs
in which no one finds time
to finish the latest exchange of being
together, where words circle back down
to what they know, newly narrowed streets,
high-rise rent, fever-blistered
arguments and squad cars stopping
and starting in memorial configuration,
remembrance moving on as ordinary
black and white. A vast restlessness
in search of newness.
This is where each morning
I surprise time and shake off sleep,
let the practiced mind relearn how
to find the day, my blue sweater and direction,
claim them like a scripture memorized

You, brother, and your two abiding loves
chose a mountain village farther south
and farther from the sea. It wasn't
a turning away from anyone as though
distance is a word for a smaller world.
It's the stocked and unstocked streams
with easy directions for learning their ways
and not losing yours in or out
but always finding tracks
that haven't been brushed away,
claiming them like your next cast

A rhythm of life and love
not troubled into believing that casting out
is like a book in the making that can actually ripen
to a flawless completion with the final words,
that best efforts are the push in the back
to perfection. No. Only a dream
of the perfect, a dream without weight,
yet too heavy for any line

The off-and-on is not done with us
or the unspooling. Not yet.
The next cast

    * *

On this river of reflections, brother,
my rod humped hard
in the middle of your telling me
you love Maclean's *A River Runs Through It*.
My rod unbent: the fish foreshortening
our catch-and-release. I reeled in,
caught unaware, checked the fly
and told you of a friend from the city
of sky-surging blast furnaces
who had to take a doctoral course with
the author: "A genuine bastard. No one
in that seminar could bear the guy's
laboured excess of put-down
arrogance." *But a genuine fisherman –*

as you back cast twice while eyeing
your mark. *With good advice*

A sudden gloom seeking its level of dark
as the wind starts up. Hesitance
of first raindrops. My eyes swim away
to elsewhere like minnows as we turn
to walk upstream from where lines and lures
trail like spent secrets on the bottom's
crisscross of timbers. It's always
the next whereabout for checking each other's
inventory and exchanging fly rods or flies
that makes a river mysterious.
We test our footing in the current
that every year breaks open another
bed beyond a shouldered bend downstream.
Unyielding high-water privilege.
You wait for me to cast, to give my line
more slack, the fly a small wrinkle
in my far-sightedness without correction:
this time almost an accidental perfection,
simple and clean release and the mark
for my next cast – three metres short
in the free flow where the river seems to run
slowly sideways before the white rush

And then you hit your spots.
Not like a target lined up with a rifle,
but something in the arm, shoulder, eyes:
farther left, right, farther out, closer,
playing out the slack for the current to take,
as always coaxing the dry fly through
a small swirl. We watch the shadow rise;
a silhouette from the deep
nudges the fly. Like the pause before
our home purchase was signed for, the slow
careful signature, how sudden it seemed
moments later. Your rod starts a wildness
silent as mere attention as you hurry in
the slack and coax the fish
through its vagaries, a rainbow
writing its unwillingness shoreward

to where you stand, the water shallow between.
A low-perched harrier on the opposite shore
squares up head and talons but stays.
This you love more than unrhymed stanzas,
and, yes, rhymed ones, and even
Maclean's haunted voice. The look side
and back, the step forward to release the fish

Good advice about that swirl.
How does one answer, if at all, and yet
for years we've traded back and forth although
I'm the one who still can use reminders
that the sudden dart of a leaf shadow
in the shallows cannot become a trout
still there somewhere in the dark,
that my line needs to breathe more slack,
that I let the fly ride the curl
of surface in and out near the far shore
close to where the current peels off
of calmer, deeper water, that I let
this cast take the measure of my next one,
and with the next one work the line
just so across a furtiveness
with a foreground of sifting light

The rain has stopped. A moment of blue
staring down, the water's pressure
running through to the unforeseen,
the rocks underfoot moving only a little.
Another cast, farther out

    * *

Brother, we both know that a faultless cast
and working of line and fly are not as easy
as losing our place, too often fooled
by accident. This continent is more
than narrowness along a shore
where ice fields and not mountain green
once issued the rivers we fish and where
cities rest uneasily on glacial till
and deep faults lines. Our land is large,

the worlds beyond much larger, and sometimes
one of us is leaving when the other
is returning with advice old and new,
the sun stalking us, conjuring shadows.
Light and dark off where we've been.
Advice is like that. Not Socrates,
not angels, not even Maclean.
In leaving and in coming home
we've watched, seen, kept going,
and tried again, as being here does

Parterres

Balance
you used to say. You meant
layout and harmony's colours,
at which you excelled,
combining long consideration
and impulsive act
with leaning on the season's good

I gardened with you, shading eyes
with red-scratched violin hands.
Now I tend simpler gardens
in Father's shirts, the ones you
offered me, no sign of darkened
age stains in the collar,
and shrunk by time to a good fit.
My days in them
have not been shabby,
and that's what I wished for you
when I said no – so you could garden
in them from hindsight laid out
like pictures on either side
of your reading machine, where
you could imagine
days to come and morning labours
in detail despite your shrinkage
of seeing to a periphery
of quarter-moon haziness

You understood
how things give out,
even the best of shirts
and vision, and yes,
the body's ways of contact
and balance
up the damp cedar steps
to your favourite garden,
the upper one

If your purpose was to reach the top
to rate results with your leftover

angle of vision, each step
will have been a silent prayer
of words half-formed and which
by themselves lacked
the usual arrangement,
like a last look back

What is left is the end
of a late summer's loveliness,
of the wonder of harmony,
of garden

The heart's parterre
ruined beyond repair

Brahms' *Requiem*

Cadences blending words, song, flesh
in the Lincoln Center's David Geffen Hall,
the many years ago leaning back
with your life, the leavings:
*alle Herrlichkeit des Menschen
wie des Grases Blumen*[1]

You: once one of the young of Yarrow
serving tea at long white tables
straight as the rows of simple graves,
the benches almost steady
as the people listen, hands cupped to hear
the hymn's title spoken,
and then, as one, join the lead singer
in four-part chorus, no songbooks,
yet every hymn at home with harmony
and grief, each phrase preparing
for the next, stanzas reckoning
beginnings and ends, reaching out
with graveyard crescendos,
dying down. Tea in the cups
no longer warm. The closing hymn's
burden guttural-deep,
pleading with faith

Hands shade eyes from the evening sun,
and some of the women brush
and brush the oil cloths with sleeves
until the men rise to a slow steadiness
and wives follow sideways,
inching steps and sway of body
to the end of the bench to leave
through the day's exit
into an evening's keeping
of heart-eating separateness
confiding in glacial soil and stones,
in root stock that probes and twists the dark.
Nothing left to wear but roots and earth.
*Ach, wie gar nichts sind alle Menschen
die doch so sicher leben*[2]

A tug at the sleeve, the need to walk
arm in arm back into the village,
where the life of country people
is laid out, waiting for them.
No names needed, merely "brother"
or "sister", often a sad belonging,
and so much to belong to,
turning away with a simple nod,
a murmur, a looking back
into the night as though daughter
and son are also coming home

Here in Lincoln Center's Philharmonic Hall
name changes and renovations still allow
assurances that draw the evening out
for any of us by filling it
with singers, orchestra and mercy,
a mercy that knows how to choke back tears
even before they form and remake
memory. A painful plenitude.
Yes, you were one of them in Yarrow

Selig sind die Toten[3] —
The end-long choral benediction.
A long hush, longer applause.
You leave to find your car,
fold yourself inside, find
bone-white lane markers in the tunnel
to the Turnpike and into oncoming
night lights, their swift skimming by
gone — with the brief avenue
of blindness. You are leaning forward

You will drive as long as you need.
You will take the *Requiem* sevenfold again
despite the shudders now and then
of lane changes, until
fugitive tollway exits weary you,
until grief tires even of itself.
You lean forward
like the people at the tables
listening for the lead singer's voice

1. "All magnificence of the human being is like flowers of the grass": from the second movement of Brahms' *Requiem*.

2. "Ah, how insignificant all humans, who nevertheless live so confidently": from the third movement of the *Requiem*.

3. "Blessed are the dead": from the seventh and final movement of the *Requiem*.

Father and Son: Cold War Harmonies

MacArthur's chutzpah howling past everything
left behind from Busan to the Yalu (after the rains
bones will push up in fields like wild flowers
and weeds). Father giving up his transport firm
to conduct choirs and teach harmony on the side,
my fingertips urging the violin into scales,
arpeggios, imperfect double stops, and then
my fifth-grade fingers explaining to Patsy in choir
that a major key can be made minor,
how slight the change, and why you don't want
a dicey new word for rhyme
in a card *valentine . . . concubine.* Miss
Lowery's one-and-two-and-three-and waiting
for our front-row whispers to find the tempo
of her pianist sister's Irish war song, feel
the shiver of its hurt deep inside the last note
tapering down to the wonder of sorrow, feel
her sister's finger brush my forehead – *this one* –
and so I joined the first sopranos of the concert choir
and sang descants with Patsy and four
braided girls, our heads and mouths like hatchlings
in a song sparrow's nest

Harmony means Bach to Brahms and pacifism –
Father's unflinching staff lines because
the new music ruins harmony like a blunted
needle on a perfectly kept LP
of the Soviet Army Male Chorus singing
"The Volga Boatmen" and "Bring the Boys Back Home"
before these find a resonance deep down
like the LP of plainchants I found for Father,
the kind you memorize *viva voce* once
you master that monophonic watch within,
and the dove on the shoulder ruffles wing feathers
against your neck, sings God's low-keyed
peace into your good ear, the one my neighbour
Barry Martin's pack of rose-red M-1s
spared, the other ear urgent as firehouse
wails and bells that will not stop for intoning
monks or textbook teachers of harmony,

even fathers who die a little each day of hunger,
the hunger of calm inside the world's roar like a bird
all to itself, following the light between thunderheads

The bells within, high and low, died away
like Angelus, but not for long, and the latest
Noise-Control Act be damned. Today
just once
let me know
what rockjazz is
let the slow-hand wary
note by note warm-up the sudden
shout of chords the fugal chase approach
the speed of let there be light and the universe
riff 'round the soul-searching anthems we sang

in Father's choirs, his polyphonic providence
between cold war furies and the silence
of those who cannot sleep or sleep forever
sounding colonnaded resonance outside the walls,
turning raucous near the buttresses, modulation
and variable measures re-composing the ache
of absence deep within into a fuller harmony.
Out there the wigwagging oxbow
curve of saxophones, the triple-tongued trumpets,
guitars, snare drums, cymbals, double bass
whoodling their ecstasy past Barry Martin's
off-key imitations of Sinatra,
past Patsy's blush and hand over mouth,
past Miss Lowery's raised hands, the glint
of her baton, past vodka pickled and pensioned
bellies of the Red Army Chorus on a Sunday stroll
along the wall, through the wall's blockade
laser-like to join choir, orchestra and holy ghosts
at the nave's far end, jam harmonies like
nothing else we've ever heard, my violin teacher
smoking sweaty plainsongs into blues
on his bull fiddle, Father twisting vowels
into falsetto and mouthing words for the singers,
locking arms with me, stomping his right foot
and weeping with joy

Natalie Marie

The late night ring of the captioned
telephone, and I turn down Schubert's
Die Winterreise. A first and second guess –
the caller ID window blank again as if
memory is a song you hear only once

I press the speakerphone button:
my daughter-in-law with
a ninth-month report that all is
as it should be. "By the way,
have you ever had the fetus listen
to classical music? This could be important
and should continue for the first five
years. At least so I've read. A friend
listens to Mozart as he works on
poems of earliest childhood memories.
He tells me their infant almost certainly
has memorized the Brandenburg Concertos
while he practiced the quaggy bottom-land
art of diaper and pajama change"

I lean closer as the telephone's active silence
finally gives in. *Baby listens to a little
of everything, Cohen, Latin swing,
Shakira, Lady Gaga, Jennifer Lopez,
Carlos Santana, old movies, your son's
moments of heavy metal and the dog's
threats to end someone's life.*
Sandrita surely knows the fetus
will have sensed ahead in her own wet way,
will have her mother's perfect hearing and good looks,
eyes shining dark as Cohen's hallelujahs,
cheeks, nose, mouth and dimples
remembering everything lured inside
the womb's acoustical chamber

and the outside that all of us need,
accepting it with a mere arm outstretched
and the slightest kick against time's headiness
toward the parting to a larger world

of moans and screams, following hesitations
into a buzz-blur of muzak
to a filmy upside down view
of five of us loudly outlined
as chorus, the solo voice recognizable

Stoically surviving crude key modulations
in the latest high-priced albums
may be in the distant offing. This
unfamiliar everything, even
time's offer of a chance to outlive
one and all of us and songs she will learn
to mouth and memorize
as a promise of the more to come.
A kind of prayer

Passport

Passport

This other language, so close
to the old Low German you and I understand,
slow-walked sheltered parts of ourselves
across wet-spotted washboard
cobblestones, through the obelisk's
pencil shade of other times, across
Amsterdam's Dam Square, swept
clean as always by slow-throttle motorized
brooms. So much mattered here
ages ago about merchants,
God's will and what we are made of.
Dissenters confessed or refused to,
Arminians, Jews and Anabaptists,
until concerned Calvinists
had whipped unmitigated free will
into hiding just in time for ancestors
to leave in the dark of centuries ago,
to let the Old Church and Royal Palace
inure the future here,
although the clock tower tolls the present
hour and Queen Juliana left the palace
and royal rule to others decades ago,
the queen who declared your uncle a rescuer
of refugees and exiles, and a knight.
There are people we know who try to be
someone else or an equivalent
when they meet each other, but he retired
to a house modest as the green hills
of Pennsylvania, in a village
where streets that begin also end,
like your visits with him

The palace bell tower still commands
air and earth for a moment's reckoning
or needless concern, like your suddenness:
I wonder when our passports expire.
We fingered them out of deep cargo pockets,
yet both of us knew these small blue
comforts have pages and years left,
unlike a refugee we met here,

his fear outfitted with envy, spent
English words and expired visa

The difference between a passport
and this chap's visa, you murmured,
is the pain still keening long after
futile study of a foreign language
at night for a place in another world.
And then another language for another place
as my father did before he simply fled
when he still could

I couldn't settle every one of your
word-by-strange-words reliving
more than mere losses, but I nodded;
I'd grown up between some of them,
and I want to know about your shirt-and-tie
father's journalistic years in Canada.
Whether any of them called heaven to witness
their own kind of free will no matter
how fateful the news arraigning days
bitten thin by attention as he proofread
once again past midnight his introduction
to the next batch of letters from refugees
he would publish tomorrow
or the day after without excuse,
without comfort

Continuum

> *So we don't need to hack a gateway in our breasts*
> *and admit these enormities.*
> Albert Goldbarth, "Mediation Song"

Our Amur maple's new-season sheen,
tenders of three-lobed leaves smooth
as the green of foothills behind the bridge's
long loom of cables weaving sky,
earth and water with what's coming:
cloud shadows the morning wants to be
free of on this day of garden warmth,
mason bees, blossoms and black
earth-shimmer of petals. Ivory flowerets
of the maple late this year
with everything else

Leafless straggler in the nursery lot's
November desolation more than
four years ago, transplanted where
our stricken apple tree had shrunk
into itself like shame, like those remaining
in Slavgorod in homes
not requisitioned after gulag
deportation lists were announced
house by house, fear filling narrow
doorways, questions beating on walls
against the loudness of semi-literacy
that mispronounced names to the last

There are seasons when hope admits
it never had a chance, for fear to follow
its wisdom into winter

There is a time
                                to follow wagons
in the dark
                                some turning off
some moving on
                                keeping distant
Cold breath

around barrenness

of trees

A voice somewhere

nailed by the night

Wide margins

around night fires

and border guards

Whispers inside you

Hands over children's

warm mouths

Get the better

of the Amur River's

chatter of new ice

Wider margins

Let the long night

of fields and sound

of rooster dawn

leave a pack horse

accountable to maggots

Learn the speech

of hands and fingers

Consider odds

of barter and quick return

One man taken

with his purchase

like dumb matter

to the perfect square

of a caravansary

Soviet uniforms

their privilege

beyond borders

like the reach

of Amur maples

measuring distance

but close as sounds

of the firing squad

from the hideout

Start again at dark

Nights bitter

with bad water

and bile

Four more

for foreign words

Docket the sun's

and their aftermath

on Shanghai's edge

of a sordid hotel

laid out on the floor

and silver fish

listening

reckoned with

in their foraging

mileposts of days

laughter of children

Short-term odds

Cold remembrance

among roaches

The consul's agent

like another casualty

Off-and-on hours of pity for others
given notice, not allowed to sail
with them across an ocean as they prayed
a ship's spangled wash of nights and days
into a single direction and first gaze
of the Golden Gate, hope finally purged
of irony and its ways of seeking cover

Journalists wrote that's what it's like
to flee from Stalin.
"They know how to get through anything"

even memory's niggling fatwa
against sleep.
In the land they had fled Kazakh muezzins
still telling the first morning light
"prayer is better than sleep"*

Counsellors advise that in hard times
one learn the art of minimal cheerlessness,
advise it to walk point around
memories of arrests a day before
the others started out, around those
betrayed after bribes were paid in full,

despair diligent as informers

There is a time beyond what came after.
Boxcar overfull. The monodrone
bruises of start and stop. Somewhere
to get to. Stench of annulment
that starts as God's will and ends
with indecorous postures of the dead,
the body's rigid outsidedness
still inside. Stop. A stepping down
that reminded them of nothing and for what?
Don't act strong. Don't act weak.
What did they know of separation, of eternal
nights filling with snow, of winter's stay
hard-set against the will to trust?

The narrow augury of root-bound
forest paths will share foreknowledge
of a namelessness where Taiga silence
sorts out the smuggled letters' quota
("remember us") and confirms
that what's real in a letter happens,
that in the gulag horror will not stop
the mind or words or drag of details,
pausing when they must to bury the dead
before yellow earthmovers are fueled,
the ones from Germany and America.
A burial prayer like the dying with
release on their lips, a fluttering
of thinned-out soul, the message returning
to itself, its years of places hidden
forever and closed to grief

                              There are seasons
with marked leavings of the lost planted
here where the winter-kill smell
of letters in the garret is almost gone,
time for our maple's roots to have wrapped tight
around the sprinkler line although rains
are generous. We on our knees, our hands
caked brown with the tree's adopted earth,
the quiet of sap inside the cambium,

bumblebees pushing the wings
of mason bees aside with rough reminders,
the maple's blossom-filigree gleaming
among its leaf-start geometry

A suddenness of clouds muscling through
the bridge towers, rush of grey and black
ignoring everything, bloating like
a migraine that eats the sky away.
The smallness of green leaf shields
still filled with light, each leaf
shivering freely in the sudden chill.
"It's coming," you standing up. "It's time."
Not yet; soon

---

*Part of the Azan, the Muslim call to prayer

Descendant

The mist against the slopes like ghosts
crowded in mountain balconies
in the far-off of evening,
as though they're all there,
souls of your dead, the missing ones,
their names still beyond reach.
It's not too late to get a few things
right – this hour and perhaps even
part of what you failed to find
in another long day's work
dying off within you, the absence
like the name that stopped
on a plausible path to the sources
to argue with you about simply
giving up

instead praising the late light's
intensity, fire in the grass,
the sun's evening warmth
that enlarges sky and shadows
with patience, fulfills them,
lets them find each other
in this valley where the talk of friends
about what's missing in their lives
keeps changing

Nightfall. Peaks of an ancient
unnamed ring of mountains
ablaze with glacial ice,
last light fading as the dark
drifts up around you,
as it gives itself entirely like
the risk of deliverance,
and you in the dark still searching
as far as you can

Abraham Wittenberg

> *Near the surface, beneath the soft penetrable mask . . .*
> *Alarm begins its troubled shoot*
>   Brigit Kelly, "Of Ancient Origins and War"

The gods who betrayed us
with winds of war,
who delivered bloated bodies
to sea shores
and left others under the rubble
of dispensations

have died. Mourners
monogrammed by travel
step slowly, bend
close, lip-read names,
including the gods', stop,
kneel down. Shapes and words
and the earth's dark rooms
have always been required,
and cold is the stone inscribed
by a living hand

Stay on your knees.
Let the damp earth
and names for the dark rooms
seep into you.
Stay on your knees and wait.
You are witnesses –

the dead all around,
an eternity kept within bounds.
But not so the genius
for great harm

Oh Abraham. Stone dead,
and your name not withheld,
the engraving deep, helpless.
The terms set long ago,
and only the gods at peace

Exodus

> *You must go on, I can't go on, I'll go on.*
> Samuel Beckett, "Unnameable"

"How can a country become a mausoleum
for innocence," he asked you the day
before artillery managed to piece him
and his white ambulance. You know how the past
repeats itself as fevered air, grief,
muffled cries and unreachable words.
You know how much there is to fear, your weanling
daughter bound to your hip again
where she can ride as dusk descends,
*if she be a daughter, she may live**
as you walk head down with others, eyes
anchored on the foreground. Somewhere

between hopelessness and the western sky
terror has kept you from turning back
even as your child watches with sidelong
curiosity those who overtake you
and pass without a glance your way,
trekking a forum of weeks like you
through time's windfalls of war and peace,
past orange and olive groves, fields
of tomatoes, artichokes, through grey
lesions of cut-away hills
and low places, over the unevenness
that leads to Europe

You know well the Qur'an's story
of how the waves crawled even closer
than the Egyptians, who almost overran Moses'
desperation. Turkey will not do so,
and at the Aegean a way opens
to let you pass through to the other side.
But unlike Allah and Aleppo's rubble
the Greeks will not tolerate your Syrian
beauty or your daughter's. Rigourously
attending to more than a thousand kilometres
to reach this shore will be held against you.

And yet you take it as a sign
that the Turkish owner of the large raft
is gone with the last of your euros, and you
have just given your last meal
to the morning red of sea swells to reach
the one-way shore coming on
to find you like a lifeline

Your balance in the shallows is co-opted
by others. A wordless man ignores your gasping
daughter, lifts you to your feet again
and step by reckless step out of your dread
of water. Sharp rocks want to wedge
your feet as if to hold you back
from the mercy of higher ground
where others in scavenged clothes have gathered
in twos and threes to share small green
oranges as though they will meet each other
again out of season, whether their clothes
are large or too small. You will soon
get your location right.
That is why you let the child grasp
your breast with a new-world hunger.
That is why you place your hand on
her streaked cheek – that unnameable feeling.
You do not notice that both of your feet are bleeding

Your mother always complained
about your play of fancy. Dreams, she said,
will stretch themselves to their limits like a vulture's
leathered wings. Your dream today:
to walk your whimpering child a month or more
westward through damp and sun-dried plains
on asphalt and well-trodden earth
with root humps and snags that test your steadiness,
into red-roofed villages
where people can be found not maimed
by age, disdain or tedium, faithful faces
and hands pledged to flesh and spirit
that span the distance between them
and you. You will ask politely for water
in English words simple as crumbs from

a daughter's broken crust, and half
understood like an old scripture.
You will ask for money for tickets
to a Berlin you've imagined ever since
the war roared its first verdict into the skirts
of your city: a full meal, more
than you can eat, with your mother's distant
cousin if you can find the no-name street
in Kreuzberg. Call it Allah's forbearance

Your destination will find you finally there
in the grittiness, pressing against the black-eyed
buzzer and the door as though the future
can be known by pushing against it,
feeling it give way as your daughter's fingers
tighten. If your relative is amazed
by all the horizons his name has hunted down,
and if he welcomes a penniless guest and her child,
you will hold back about family and friends,
mindful to listen with greater care
than he to mark and memorize
words in the endless rush of German
that with the beggarly packet of your papers
can reach out to those in charge of separateness
when they ask who you really are

The loudest voices among the nations have said
to each other you wouldn't dare come this far.
Those first silver strands of hair, their evidence
of memories prepared to harm, will prove
the voices wrong, and given the chance, you
will share with them your way of unsaying,
since there is nothing else

---

*Exodus 1:16, Everett Fox translation

Learning Turkish

Not my yellow pocket-sized
phrase book, not the airline magazine's
glossy bilingualism, nor
the white-glove pro bono attentions
of flight attendants.
Not even the driver's reckless steering
and bitten off questions
in English-German-Turkish
brought me any closer
than a vulture's unalterable circles
that give the sun a wide berth
under the sky's blue roof

The sun loops dust
among intermittent shadows
of pink oleanders.
September colour, prickly heat,
glare and squint. Remoteness
is searching for the intermittent
outpost barks
of a bored dog

The new road veers away
from the village.
Here, on the old-road precedence
of small stone cottages,
a few without a roof,
a young woman sits forward,
widow's weeds spilling over
body and stool, hooded head
bent toward
a congery of blood-red jars,
her right hand searching through
her loose leather bag. Searching

My best wishes and request
need the help of hands, fingers
and mispronunciation
for me to pay for a litre
of pomegranate essence,

more than enough
for the seasons to come –
and I bid her goodbye.
A nod as she looks down
to her shadow, a belonging
that holds her here,
fingers still rummaging
her oversized purse
as if to grasp for this moment,
for a lifetime sagging in on itself,
what can't be understood
except as dumb astonishment
of betrayal

The Cow of Good Fortune:
A Prose Poem on Non-Fiction

For Tamera

It's your fierce whispers that redden the large cow circling us head down, dripping water from her mouth, tossing her head up as if she's had enough to drink, eyes wide apart to watch me swallow your ink-black rasps of Turkish and English and pauses frightened by the cow's nearness as we move closer. The dream trying to explain itself before completing its work and already forgetting what it wanted to explain, except you, my daughter, ask again for the value of that part of a cow tired and angry enough with everything, including the boy, to stop circling, lie down on her side, end this dream and die among village onlookers in their everyday Turkish drab rather than turn and walk in her usual lane of life, leaving me elsewhere, not in Lycia but on Yarrow Central Road, a boy who watched the cows from the common pasture grow large, file by close as their smell in a rhythm hoofing the gravel loose, thwacking each step, every head bobbing as though not part of the herd or a village of small barns, and yet part of remembering, tails ruddering them forward as if to help hold the line. Then one or more veer suddenly away from the others with a slight nod and turn in to their yard and gate, udders slapping sideways

i

We agree: take the old road home for the view, the Aegean concentrating pure turquoise below my side of the car from Kadikalesi to Turgutreis, gulls etching the sea in their slow pursuit of each other and farther back islands riding arc-lines of surf filled with light. From Turgutreis to Akyalar, where we turn into the hills to Gürece: sun-seared slopes to the left, the ridge treeless, sun hanging from a cloud's vast aureole, your window wide open despite the air conditioner's snuffle, half of my window a dust-spangled brilliance. I want to say *taking a local bus would have been easier* as we slow, steer through herds of cloud shadows, pull visors down as the road doubles back through yellow-flowered prickly pear, past evergreen domes of maki and half-hidden huddle of stone houses, the sag of their roofs, the grey stitchwork of stone hedges . . .

    A boy, thin as bamboo and much too close

running toward the cow in front of us, its red head and neck
turned to face us as she lifts with a whump and swims our way
from the road's mirage, nose widening its blackness toward
us, flattening against the windshield like a bird's hapless fate,
weariness staring past everything. When a cow's eyes slide
from a car's hood they leave nothing behind except front end
damage until the door offers more than asphalt: the cow on its
side, larger than it was, as we step out, as trepidation increases
redness, as a beat-up truck tries to steer around us, the boy's
words following his hands to explain that he untied the cow
and turned his back, the cow convulsing, shitting on weather-
eaten pavement in steady rhythm, around her neck a rope with
the blue eye to guard against evil, witnesses gathering, closing
in on our doubts that we're really here, wanting to know why.
Since neither of us has answers, they have theirs', eye-level
rage become meticulous, your back to me, your head turned,
mouth hand-cupped for a loud whisper asking what a cow is
worth. The shouting will not be shut out, but the question waits,
bending the years far back from here to dairy herds in Yarrow.
The police chief, the one known for hurting young women in
his jail, arrives like a mirror's reflection of sagging eye bags
and belly and an intensity of smiles for us all. Our artless offer
is rejected, and he writes and writes, *for another time* you
mutter next to my good ear ringing with words foreign as any
time and place where not a single word wanted to be heard.
And neither you nor the police chief nor the crowd's chorus of
exactions notice the red mass of convulsions yield to shivers,
the cow stuttering up hind end first on her third try and starting
a slow circle almost true, her radius from an unknown centre,
a four-legged limp round the ragged ring of people gathered
to confirm their hard life like the cow's, beyond redemption,
the cow's circling like a search for coming back from not being
lost, body almost together, jerking herself forward, each step
more expected, a more certain rhythm, head turned to us as if
figuring all of us out, deaf to the car-horn bedlam behind us

Not a single gaze at our Ford's hollowed-out hood or the red
and black Galatasaray soccer flag limp on the aerial's tip. But
everyone knows a cow cannot be struck twice, and the owner

can't help the twitch in his smile – how miracles and windfall are really the same. When the cow dips her head to muffle a snort our offer is accepted: 350 dollars in Turkish lira for a cow milked morning and evening (600 if her milk has dried and 800 if she dies before tonight) – the cow still circling and circling us, gnats feasting on our stickiness of drying sweat

The truth about a red cow's halting orbits of head-bobs on a far-gone road in southwestern Turkey is this: if a young woman walks back to her company car to find her purse and her father walks with her, wary of the policeman's short white sleeves, hairy arms and fat index finger varying his theatre of bidding cars by on stones and grit of the shoulder, the cow will have gone when they return, and if they look where others are looking, the cow, loosed from everything except direction, is mincing up the road through heat-waves, head still hitching, tail a private back and forth like a pendulum's recitation of a day's regular advance, our eyes and the boy following as she sways into her yard, her long rope lurching behind like misery

ii

It happened, we say. Not as a hit during a slap-happy tourism of hits and mostly misses, the hits without damages and with pictures to prove them. It happened thirty years ago as if in a dream parallel to a life really lived with all its name changes, even changes now lost as memory tries to redeem place and shape of what's been lost. I'm told you and I are much alike, long-term memory loyal as we try to tell how it happened to us or to the others or to the cow, how the cow rose from the sun-baked road rump first like a wonder, recalled by something deep within. Will any of the others watching with anger have searched themselves without anger for details that have gone missing? Memory, like a cow's redness, can circle and circle as intently as Brigit Kelly's three cows and the moon, and this stand-up yet unsteady circling is what heaps up large measures of detail, welcome or not. Sleep is often far yet near with them, with an imprint of their tenacity on particulars and arrangement. Hit or miss, we don't ask why try to save again and again what saved itself or can't save itself in the whoosh of time. It's not us remembered; it's remembering. It's torn-off pages of our world still filed within us, including the partialities of damaged

scraps, their desire to survive. Sometimes unsteady circling
is like a letting go. Sometimes almost too much returns with
gratitude or fear, assembled into what's entirely recognizable
as if we managed every part and the whole, and even today we
walk away from what almost broke us down and retell it as
"this, more or less," details tallied as though damages provide
lucidity that can be shared in different versions, although the
cow got up on her own, the boy changed his story and the
policeman's report said you turned the wheel to hit the cow

Today's new road from Turgutreis and Akyalar is four lanes
wide, you've built new offices in Bodrum, you use a driver
mostly, your police chiefs can be trusted, at least the ones
we know, and the price of cows has gone through the roof
with everything else like trees in your atrium. Never have you
haltered the word unlucky or let it get away, but neither of us
will forget the jailed half-night for ransoming a pregnant cow

Inventory

The deck rail's varnish seizes all it can
from the sun as pine bees nose forward
on the curvature, stumble, lose hold,
lurch back into the shine,
buzz each other's wings out of the way.
The soft thump-thump of dinghy
against stern keeps time
with our gulet's slight rocking
inside the turquoise curl
of water where sea perch
rearrange the bottom of sand and grass
like rungs of a long ladder
shelving the sand six metres down

Familiarities joined as one –
Cape Triopion afloat
on a vast crease of light,
the distant dock, the bowl of land.
The mainland climbing high
out of the greatly changed
ruins we remember

      **

There are changes so sudden each seems
a given but the yields don't agree,
not even on facts
such as a false forecast and survival
on the open Aegean. On engine power
yesterday we lowered sails, the jib
half way, as the rigging began to sing
and groan in a trumpet-tongued gale's
outbursts, as the sea troughed blacker,
deeper, and on the slopes of teetering swells
lacework of foam broke faith
and flew by like new snow in a
high plains blizzard. Screams of water
and salt untied the jib, ripped it
like mourning cloth, shrouding
the bowsprit as sea rushed the deck

bow to stern, starboard to port
in its indiscriminate searches,
the diesel surging, relenting,
our deck hand missing.
The radio's whistles and hysterical stutters
and the pump's chug-chugging hollowness
hurried me to gather and hold jib
and my fear, to wrap them tightly around
the spar, tie them with loops and clove hitch
as the spar reared up
before plunging beneath the wave
in a fierce testament of repetition,
a fatefulness feeding it without end,
and the loops beginning to loosen

Had the deck hand, down to dry heaves
below, looked out the porthole glass,
he would have known it's no calmer
there than where the chairs swept
off the deck and danced for a moment
on a swell before vanishing
in the long white gleam of a wild sea,
the only certainty a waiting out
for what that gleam would yield, a gleam
that takes its time like a change of sky
or advice that deals with the mystery
of danger where we find it and not
with rescuing what's been lost or figuring
the cost of what we want or what, if anything,
can still be done

    **

Melville's Starbuck would have no one
in his crew who knew no fear.
That is why his words were gentle, even
on days when mere air couldn't bear
any more of a vast ocean's chaos
drowning out defiance or nonchalance
and quickly closing over innocence.
And yet his fear-encrusted bravery
could not outlast his qualms,

could not take the will for the deed.
Fear, an unwritten part of our inheritance,
no matter how old the testament

Here on the sheltered side of the isthmus,
not far from where the ancient Knidos
is being reassembled piece by piece
on Triopion and the mainland
like the desiccant bones of Ezekiel's
prophecy, the deck hand is bringing up
the few surviving white plates and goblets
from the galley. He would rather not say
anything, and we speak little to each other
or to him of yesterday

No one says we'll do better next time,
and only one says that on the whole
everything held and what didn't can easily
be restored or, like gratuitous forecasts,
can be done without. It's as if
nothing we tried made much of a difference
in the vast fury of the storm,
its winding down, or after the fact.
Except that we are moored at Knidos,
docking lines tied fore and aft,
and we have screaked the mainsail half way up,
then down again, the sun heaving gently
east and west, the horizon unsteady.
A morning's seaworthiness, but memory
plays the storm for time enough to undo
every loop and knot

The Acropolis of Assos/Behramkale, Turkey

After the corpses' gluttony of positions
at Çanakkale and the broad eddies of blood
overrunning the sea like oil at Izmir,
after the designs of nations broken
like wings and legs of pelicans by mirages,
after people cleansed themselves
of each other with binge and purge of words
that weary-winged empires had worked toward
for years, after the murder of many who left
or stayed behind, God gave the Greeks
the turquoise sea and Turks the land
with sea enough for brine-eaten rows of iron cleats
and nets and creels on the wharf, set out to mend
in front of stone-and-mortar hotels
and red pantiled roofs

And after old dialects and alphabet
were confiscated for softer sounds
and harder loyalty to a new mode
of remembrance, past as semblance of the future

ancient retaining walls behind the harbour
of Assos still eat into the gradient like old griefs
to keep some things as they were, and into
a ribbon of road along the walls, greying
with asphalt corrugations, the car torsioned
like a dinghy caught by sea swells.
The route climbs sunlight past archaeologists
who have stopped to let the morning hit up against
another day of digging out the Roman
road and the Greek arterial close beneath it.
Our way climbs to the smooth manifold
of a plane curve inviting infinity
but finding coordinates from half-buried
sarcophagi on the treeless steep,
the ancient necropolis where the world's heaviness
heard the treacheries of voices deep inside
the earth, and the slope shook itself
past the walls, as if there's always more,
as if nothing is real until it's covered

up, as if to house the past for a road
to pass over before yielding to straight
into the town's geometry of unnamed alleys.
An unlikely one argues itself higher and higher
around rocks, maki and shrivelled
melissa, through mountain tea, brown
spear grass and thyme's sweet breath
to the rockbound edge of our search,
an acropolis against the sky,
where young boys leap with the mathematics
of angels from pillar segment
to ruined capital and entablature,
over the local boredom of millennia,
over the marbled breasts of the slave holding high
a trencher emptied eons ago, over
the high-hand commands of gods broken
like everything else, the leaps more daring
over us down on our knees, over and back,
and we step aside, look farther around

So much sun from Athena's ruined temple
all the way to Lesbos, the Aegean surf
below, each moment washing forward
into the next, the past running
ahead, looking back at what will come

Long before Athena's favourite forsook
the far-off region of his mind and warned
against the new religion, and long before
Paul walked the Roman road down to the harbour,
unsure that a body painful as his
will ever be pure spirit, Aiolians gathered
as usual on this foreland, sang Sappho's songs
by heart, as many as they had memorized, but some
said tomorrow to the one ready to recite
the soliloquy of ruin all Lesbos knew –
of the north Aegean marauding murderers,
Achilles and his men. The vast anthology
of stars waiting for the moon to rise
over Troy, its level after charred level,
not many miles away

The Bosporus

You could have started elsewhere later,
warmth and sound fattening everything.
Where you stand Asia and morning
do not ask if you are willingly chilled.
But from here you can look all around
at the ghostly real. To the right
the northern mouth of the Bosporus
smoking dawn's red breath
and a sea's black entrance
silent as underwater ruins

Someone calls once from the slope
behind and above, and there was a time
when you might have answered regardless
of who was calling whom. You have learned
to watch without words until the words
find you like the lights' sudden-on
to your left in the restaurant of red trumpet flowers
and windows mirroring the latitude of wakefulness.
Ahead, at the top of stairs where the railing begins,
a sign's warning (*Dikkat*) of dangerous steps
down, the three-word behest
showing through a maze of graffiti colours

On the opposite shore bluffs and villas begin
to form in the groping shimmer and shadow
of seafront margin somnambulating
into view with moments of half-hidden
mansions unsure of how far to crowd
down to the water line.
The shore of Europe just inside of time

You watch a main street sea-to-sea channel
freighted with commerce
that bears new worlds as well as old
vaguely along, their deep currents
of cross purpose and grievance
never exhausting themselves
or a need of countless wars to store up
memories of how to keep things apart,

urging days and years to be on watch

The spine's memory board alive:
yesterday as evening opened itself
to the black smudge of tankers
coming and going low in the water
or riding high with rust past puny
fishing boats returning to their jetty,
one day less in their life, the late hour
befell you with a sign of the times
as with "if this had been a real emergency" –
immaculate grey of a stars-and-stripes frigate
of the future and its escorts of war
and peace gliding past the muezzin's wail
with hardly a sound, ignoring the call to prayer
as you watched an argosy's wake
subside into a sea's wide reach

And minutes ago the mist gave way
to perfectly large white numbers and the Russian
tricolour: missile-fitted destroyer, sailors in place
like small chess pieces ready for the next
match, a heavily laden war-worn
transport fuming close behind,
its slim freeboard margin focusing the mind
on more than Archimedes' principle.
The Turkish Coast Guard following
in the wide trough of swells,
parsing this passage with binocular strictness
and a red-trim-on-white reminder

Following like you as the sun yellows
upward through the mist to its own side
of day. This world, so much older
than you, so settled, so unsettled,
has found you with its leftovers
of past and present, "chance being
at one with choice."* The sun rises
on your readiness to name what's here,
to rename remainders, especially
unspeakable ones. And it's you who steps
forward to the sign at the stairs

and beyond. This morning does not tempt
whatever will be to harbour more than destinations,
but in an hour or two people will crowd
the Bosporus, and only some of them
will know how indifferent rage of empires
and intimacies of genocide have always
begun as an ending, as its base line

_____

*From Yeats' "Solomon and the Witch"

Amazons

The future's dream of the past
billeted on underlayers of legend
is not without uneasy quietus
of rumours whose wounds are closed
or healing still

The present can be like that
as well as a king's surviving warriors
a mere month after the screams
of a queendom's horseback Amazons
in formations designed for an end
to things as they had been turned the day:
gallop, storm of screams, sword, clamour
of bronze on bronze, arms too easily giving
their blood, breath bubbling, broken bodies
taking their shadows down with them
until the men fled. And not far away,
the god of war remembering everything

When the Amazons packed tents, hides
and queen and led their horses to better water
the men moved with the blandishment
of contrition, beguilement, and unrelieved distance
in the same direction until the women spoke
with their hands, each warrior beckoning a young man
into her tent, and there was peace, the future
holding its breath as if to question whether
fugitive survivors can be right about anything,
and yet in the evenings the breeze long as time
counted the years this side of extinction.
But after centuries the women warriors
ceased to be ordinary. A story spread
in kingdoms known for brokering vassalage
of how Amazons cut away the breast
on their dominant side when they come of age
so as to teach the body the lesson of how
pain identified by scars betters violence
even before it finds the enemy. A one-breasted
fiend willing to sleep with you, grooming
you to prepare meals and care for

the children when she went away to war

Here in Ereğli, east of the Golden Horn's
beginnings reborn as Byzantium,
we imagine the Black Sea's far shore,
how a queendom of Amazons
left stone house clusters behind here
for time's unroofing and burial, how
they awakened wars far beyond
these rope twists of clouds and two fishermen
in their homely boat, white shirts
filling and emptying as morning
exaggerates light on the vast field of water
and terns turn as one toward the sun
above the wind-serrated surface

We sniff out the breeze, choose the lower
terrace to walk any lingering innocence
and morning hunger to table and chairs.
Our hostess starts down on the half-naked
path of sand and grass: a striding sense
of casualness through the shadows' undertow,
a broad full-bodied, full-breasted
privilege. Yesterday screams at her husband
lingered longer than the smoke billowing
from the kitchen, and she seized his faint
muttering mid-sentence,
then silence after evening had been
fully served and night settled down

Gneiden. We return her oncoming
"good morning." She is here with
three kinds of cheese, a pomegranate
she breaks with her hands for us,
freshly cured olives, tomatoes,
melon slices like flames of tangerine orange,
arugula, and eyes dark for what happens given time,
their sword-flash of light.
Her husband will serve the tea

The bougainvillea that holds
the stone inn's change of tone front

and side is red as last evening's wine
on the house

As If

"We Strongly Prefer Experimental Verse"

Your sight is better than your hearing,
and trouble can come of that
when the chandeliers of the theatre's
half-dark find a head of frizzled orange
and green by halves three seats over
cradling a tower of coat-folds,
program glints, paperback,
stilettos and bucket hat.
A small lurch into the back of her seat
pulls them closer, a slight tilt,
but they ride in place
with her closed eyelids
as the violin's cadenza
of a body's disarrangement
outdoes the conductor with
its very own atonal fury/
pizzicatos/faint caterwaul of bow
upside down on all four strings/
loud knock on wood/and skating
to the bridge on the E string
at the speed of stage lights crosshatching
the syncopation of violin
and heads crowded close in front

The tower leaning more by fractions
toward Pisa, her movement mute,
uncommissioned, unrehearsed,
yet breathtaking as Dame Evelyn Glennie's
perfect percussive balance double dared
by the kettle drum's blunder in the pause
and the orchestra's final home to havoc
exploding in disaccords, crash
of silence, intermittent
ripples of applause

Local Television News

No. You don't want to say "come in, please"
to wind-blown hair
and eyes too bright for the weather.
Open the door and she might mount
the final step and measure your jaw
with a microphone
too large for her hand. She might
stalk you around books on your
living room floor like a golden retriever
in the inter-lake marshes,
shivering with readiness

But you can't bug her off the yard
as with a scamming roofer
and other close friends of township jails.
Not that neon yellow dress
and purl-knit neckline pretending modesty
on the second-highest step

Through the pinch of light
below the Venetian blind
you watch a derelict parking metre
between your car and hers interview
a black-bristle mutt,
head very large, legs very short;
and half way to the door
the camera man's cigarette
smokes its way through today's list

which started here because
your brother-in-law shot through the eye
of a saliva-drooling coyote on the lawn
with your pellet gun as your schnauzer
yipped from behind the porch rail
like an evangelist.
Your fibreglassed right arm
and shoulder feeling everything

You, almost unlucky as the coyote,
hate cigarette smoke,

but you too have lists, some forgotten,
fewer written down, items spaced
for possible additions, and pages
struck through top to bottom
like City Code regulations
no longer enforced, your saving grace

And who knows, some of your lists
may all along have been sharing information
on the dishonour of forgetting,
of growing older,
the kind of information
withheld by the shameless magenta
of the TV screen's off-centre
MUTE, which stays where it is,
and you refuse to move
from your chair by the closed blind

getting better by the day

Boredom

it's my assistant. He kept the manuscript
for more than an unmemorable year
after the promise of a speedy decision
that misspelled your name
twice: she's *charmed by any tree's seasoned*
come-hither even those in a zen meditation
or as longsome life force in city
or country graveyards or as margins
left and right in landscape paintings
Lower case leading the way, the unsaid
and punctuation implied

And he's tired of it all, the bad as well
as the good. Time can do that, days
coursing through what the years beheld
with unattended weariness and, for that matter,
wayfaring through your manuscript:
the opening section may well leave readers
as lost as speakers in your monologues
except perhaps for the one
on your late father's office mess
Each re-reading he fell asleep, awakening
somewhere in the main section,
the longest poems, all of them on trees
and you among them
some moments here and there but still
a parade of pretexts for private interests
to wit autobiography in disguise
and aimless travelogue as collateral
He doesn't say damage

Regardless of how your name is really spelled,
the small space between any second
thoughts and a reply has been closed
like windows of a barely breathing room
because sustaining air is no more
of account. And not the boredom of doodles
in a book you won't keep or of outsized
black marker ads in the window
of Aberna's store. You are thinking

stage-four metastatic boredom

The fact drowsing, already settled in
the factor, not needing to be implied.
In the Mona Lisa the implied is in the smile,
for Schoenberg in the long-term memory
of the diatonic, in dendrology texts
habitual hints of ancient Greek.
And in the REM of lounge-chair sleep
it's the eye movements refusing to follow
as the manuscript withdraws soundlessly
on its right-of-way from half-open hand
to thigh by degrees and onward with
barely breathing caesuras, glancing lightly
against the knees before disassembling,
the order unprotected, falling past
everything. Falling forever

Descartes and Rumours of a Plague

That spooky space between one's feet
and the earth, between
the step-by-step undoing
of mismatched sheets
tangled on the line
and the gravity of the sag,
the long latitudinal white between
"maybe" and the almost illegible
"not," the overlap
of principle and principal,
a yawn and what I infer
is your "I suppose/propose yes"

I know I think, but I'm not sure
of the reason we reason, or what
follows, or the reason why some say
weather dictates whether we think
as others or think for ourselves.
I am, however, done with packing
for the countryside
much earlier this year,
my portmanteau hardly half full

Ode to Horace

Sometimes he wept when he reminded her
of what hasn't stayed yet stays. He meant
history's lively mirroring, the ode,
first breathed into life by Pindar
and Horace, and after Horace left the safety
of the ancients to ride centuries
of expectancy all the way to Keats
and beyond before tapering away
like the gods. Yet still awaking willful
        sureties into life

Years of the front-row students who knew
his sit-down lectures as a congress
of vestige, oracle and the immortal
enjoining their desires of a sequel.
One always dressed in yellow cap; her
admiration for oracles so passionate
        he left his wife

He rued the history of odes templed
as lost legacy. And Virgil's "dark
memory of time"* mustered his
"untimely", the voice searching for
itself. He doesn't hear his young wife
swallow the rest of "your retirement"
as she rises and he sinks into himself,
light fingering through the blind, limning
the hand that presses the perfect spine of Milton's
Latin odes, the book's boards spread.
The mentoring of the Commonwealth and hell
face down but learned by heart and line
seeking to regain what time forfeited,
shapes of a world true as a soul restored.
The Redemption of Time he titled his book
        thrice reviewed

The only movement his daylong jacket,
shoulders – sleeves – cardigan, slumping
themselves into the back of the stuffed chair
that long ago confirmed his lineaments,

the breathing and centuries of ventriloquists
as saviours speaking for themselves
and him for what should happen in a poem
of the world or the world of the poem.
            Measures of surety

These unbroken cadences of beauty
amid broken expectancy. Milton
still face down like the slippers,
socks a near match. It's women
that change, that wash away life lines
of a well-wrought marriage. Her yellow cap
long gone. Perhaps she married him
without intending to. Exactly when
did she begin to question poetry's highest
good, her new idiom seeking mere
            momentariness?

A tentative presence as though she doesn't live
here anymore. A presence still feeding
beauty and memory, but clothed again
this morning in the sinewy black of
her cohort of women. She opens wide
the door; a different light takes over,
framing her hurried look his way, closing
his eyes. Will she return to serve the dinner
tonight? The room drawing in breath,
            holding it. Yes

*And it's not about the mouse or spread
of mould or the radiator gasps.
It's not about you exactly. It's
the willfully abiding innocence,
the lingering everything, the gullibility,
ours, our nation's, the moral disrepair.
Yes, I'm still marching; we will march
the entire year at intersections, all
         of them*

---

* Virgil's *Aeneid*, Book IX

Journal of the Plague Years

Fear

Neither your breakfast cough
nor the intangible dreams between
your night intervals
or the latest body count
have helped you herd his fears
into submission

and letting him by first
as you open the door
to step outside in time for
your usual survey
is not an act of assurance

There is little to see,
outline and shape gone.
You inhale and exhale
the cold morning fog
as deeply as you can

but you are losing
the argument;
you are breathing the air
he just exhaled

Ballad of the Plague Years

with a debt to David Abram

Because the people
speak of an end
coming like a thief in the night
how night will take
many more bullets
and then the day of reckoning
when bodies washed
and buried this year
will rise like a cry
from out of the ground
with all that was
clinging to them

he changed his question
from what is coming
after the end
to what will come
of evening news
and whether she
was really a healer
or merely another
airbrushed fill-in
for star-lit gods

I don't work miracles
she said
and sometimes hope
wears me out
especially now
that the night
is here
and many are sure that the dark
will afflict them
with what we worked
all day to heal

Temper of the Times

"I felt it getting ready yesterday.
The order I sign today will say
we began, frankly, before it started,
and we will control it once and for all.
This year will be much better;
others will die the death they wished
for us. All of us have a part to play.
My advisors will arrange a meeting
to salute those who stand with us
and those who work the graveyard shift"

Shadow darts of swallows on a car
empty as the shine overtaking
nothing, not even the onlooker
who has stopped for the scream of an ambulance
delivering miles of slowly fading
life left to a silence as indignant
as the press secretary's closed captions
guttering in the store-front glass

In this city's afterlife of heatwaves
a woman rushes across the street,
no traffic, no gestures,
but once on the other side
she begins to walk away as though
remembering only what didn't happen,
as though this morning is a getaway
to anger

Reality Show Samson

The monotony of your daily recriminations,
she used to say. A compulsion.
You couldn't ignore her wordless scorn
for your endless drone of distractions,
her figure still beautiful, the eyes
clear and round as the room
watching you. The clumsiness
of your restlessness has never known
the body's real language

And no apologies for what you did to her,
your second chance gone
like the sinews of your celebrity hair
and your adulterous eyes' satisfactions
in rooms smoky from adjectives
of blandishment that can break
the pubescence of angels.
An ache of absence still there,
alone now,
but a different hunger long chained
within you slipping free
to buy you time: to stop her affair
with your enemies and end
the court orders against you

Eyes of blue
and deeply puckered retinas,
you grope gilded door plate and knob
the years memorized for you,
tall palms of your resort
a puzzle of sound
like a guess about to get it wrong
as you ponder your chances:
the gains and losses that remain,
how much can still be shaken loose
from your wasted years
and the rage that held the balance
of what you built back then
and all that was built for you
pillar to post

These yearnings in your shoulders,
Samson, how lonely
your whispers: "It never was her.
I could stand in the middle of 5th Avenue.
I am strong. There is still time."
You always said you're not afraid.
The sign in the new Dollar Store says
Everything You Lack.
Is it that you never really had
what's needed now?

If You Look that Way

Back-on-the-maskless-show exhilaration
as he spreads his legs in the largest chair
and leans toward the stage lights
to gather an assortment
of anodized smiles from the host's greeting
and borrow from the buddy system
of speech alphas – incisor response
ready, communion of cocky cadences
charming the edge of every pause
searching out the next move
against a nation with foreign accents,
a people of every sort of sex,
and wayward pilfered votes in plain
view if you look that way

A change of voice like a garment rending:
the hidden hand in zig-zag storms
and their leavings among unroofed suburbs,
in trailer parks on their sides.
And science has been handed its final solution,
the hum of refrigerated trucks
behind the ER, their prior claim
as clear as the Lord's I-told-you-so
nod and the stretch-marked cheeks
and forehead or the contract
for his next book, just confirmed

along with the moment for miracles,
this tiding, too, not self-forgetful.
Soon, very soon – simplicity
of arms raised past themselves
as if to roll up the curtain between
the world's deep dark
and pale light already glimpsed
in the under edge of the creeping up,
an offer of a secret ready
to reveal itself,
his arms a little higher as he
turns to watch us watching him

The Quiet of the Field

The lock-down not over, I wonder
like others what I have lost.
Surgical mask below my chin,
I stand sentry in the roadside
grass, tracking the far-off crawl
of tractor, disc-harrow and dust
as the horizon separates
and draws them on over the bench
of hill below clouds that remake
loopholes into an open-and-close
of blue, there again, and giving out

A skein of light streams up the hill,
as tractor and rider reemerge
from the far side, etching the field's
suddenness of fragile sunstruck
glory with a black shining
that follows in a seam on
the move, unzippered, a light and dark
station-to-station crossing over
like memory slowly repeating itself.
The methodical growl of a truck passes
behind me, its whisk of wind too close.
The sucked-in breath –
I turn back to the quiet of the field:
light narrows to a razor-edge
phosphorescence
retreating as a bright new relinquishment
to a darkening foothill haze of green
and colour-drained slopes of Mount
Tahoma, the mountain's headdress
and cloudship canopy prophesying
storm

Sooner or later farmers, weather,
mutating pathogens,
and the seasons themselves are in a time
of prophecy
(for every prophecy there is a season),
and we are in it – inside our voices

pulling predictions dead ahead
in firm lines, darkening outcomes
in a world of hacked warning systems

This day began alone, nothing
to make up to what has been
and will be,
and it may not be long enough
once more to teach me quiet,
that purest of loves, easily lost
and therefore always new, ready
for what happens when no one
is here to watch with me.
The still small breath of aloneness
that even the imperfect heart
knows, a passionate quiet
that will not last, yet comes again.
The breath full enough

A Mere Morning Walk

They say they have everything to do with us,
these unlucky ghostings.
"The OFF button, please!" My wife and I
zip up and step outside behind our masks
onto the morning's stage
with what life-belittling has left us
besides our feigned indifference of fear.
Yesterday the street an unswept
vacancy tracking a stranger
looking back, an ongoing watch as if
the emptiness might overtake him,
and then the bat jetting through
our open door, its wall-to-wall careening
like a spirit desperate to be found

Hand on each other's shoulder curve,
a morning rite, we frown as usual
at our neighbour's unsettlement
of molehill-freckled lawn,
daze of dandelion pom-pons, loops
of wild blackberry briars overeager
to strangle the posted *No Trespassing* sign
and reach into his house, which,
he'd promised us, would go down with him.
But here, between the postal box and
inching hum of bees in the red valerian sprawl,
a newer sign with altered face,
a diagonal overscript of *Sale Pending*

No one can tell we're smiling past
surprise and past the crosswalk to people
gathered in twos to reason the slight mark
of a rear-end impact through inference
from foreknowledge and after, not
drawing themselves in at our approach,
and we not juddering them to the curb
with our own aging balance
as if flesh above all is to be avoided

Stopping to measure the moment

with a half-hidden embarrassment
of curiosity can be a way of greeting among
the least of us disguised as routine
walkers "going onward the same"* —
you and I nothing more than life-long
lovers now hand-in-hand nodding departure
and once again reconciling length
and pace of stride through mixed housing
even as a dog who has not learned the art
of separation seeks to befriend us
almost all the way to the end of the road
at the cliff's overlook
of sea and the glacier-hooded slopes
of Mount Tahoma steadfast to a fault

How strange to get so near each time
to the warning *No One Beyond This Point*.
The elements of morning
here are composed, not traces
from the dawn of life, merely a kind
of writing over the earth's molten core,
tracing the latest edgy moves
of the Pacific plate, updating
a continent, a volcano's slumber
and an ocean's vast leftover restraint.
Small waves ride their calm to the shore
beyond the handrail, sure as this rock face
high above a wavering and plunging
of seabirds, their sudden wheeling
past gravity, their tenuous shadows
scattered by the surface

There are sudden moments like this
in stories not leaving things out,
moments barely distinguishable
from secret folds of faith. Far off
at the sky's faint edge of no return
a cloud floats out of itself

---

* From Thomas Hardy's "In Time of 'The Breaking of Nations'"

www.ingramcontent.com/pod-product-compliance
Lightning Source LLC
Chambersburg PA
CBHW070940080526
44589CB00013B/1582